coolcareers.com

Computer

Animator

Annie O'Donnell

the rosen publishing group's
rosen central
new york

Published in 2000 by The Rosen Publishing Group, Inc.
29 East 21st Street, New York, NY 10010

Copyright © 2000 by The Rosen Publishing Group, Inc.

First Edition

Library of Congress Cataloging-in-Publication Data

O'Donnell, Annie.
    Computer animator / Annie O'Donnell. — 1st ed.
        p.   cm. — (Coolcareers.com)
    Includes bibliographical references.
     Summary: Introduces the field of computer animation, describing various jobs in this field and training and education needed to get them.
        ISBN 0-8239-3101-3
    1. Computer animation—Vocational guidance Juvenile literature. [1. Computer animation—Vocational guidance. 2. Vocational guidance.] I. Title. II. Series.
TR897.7.036   2000
006.6'96'024—dc21   99-41826
                                                          CIP

Manufactured in the United States of America

CONTENTS

ABOUT
THIS BOOK

Technology is changing all the time. Just a few years ago, hardly anyone who wasn't a hardcore technogeek had heard of the Internet or the World Wide Web. Computers and modems were way slower and less powerful. If you said "dot com," no one would have any idea what you meant. Hard to imagine, isn't it?

It is also hard to imagine how much more change and growth is possible in the world of technology. People who work in the field are busy imagining, planning, and working toward the future, but even they can't be sure how computers and the Internet will look and function by the time you are ready to start your career. This book is intended to give you an idea of what is out there now so that you can think about what interests you and how to find out more about it.

One thing is clear: Computer-related occupations will continue to increase in number and variety. The demand for qualified workers in these extremely cool fields is increasing all the time. So if you want to get a head start on the competition, or if you just like to fool around with computers, read on!

chapter one

A HISTORY OF COMPUTER ANIMATION

Whether you know it or not, you've seen lots of computer animation. Animation—the word means "bringing to life" or "giving movement to"—is artwork that involves moving objects and characters, such as the ones in cartoons. The talking animals and flying cars that you see in TV commercials, the wild special effects in movies like *Star Wars: The Phantom Menace,* and maybe even your favorite video are all examples of computer animation. But computer animation and computer art have been around a lot longer than you might think.

The first forms of computer-aided art were created as early as the 1950s, when artists would program points—coordinates that represent a position on a computer screen or piece of paper—into computers using key punch cards

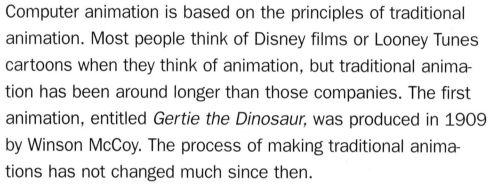

and output their work onto paper
using a pen plotter.

TECHNICAL DEVELOPMENTS ▶▶▶▶▶▶▶▶▶▶

Computer animation is based on the principles of traditional
animation. Most people think of Disney films or Looney Tunes
cartoons when they think of animation, but traditional animation has been around longer than those companies. The first
animation, entitled *Gertie the Dinosaur,* was produced in 1909
by Winson McCoy. The process of making traditional animations has not changed much since then.

In traditional animation, the animator draws each scene,
or frame, on a cel, a piece of transparent (see-through)
acetate, which is a type of plastic material. In each consecu-
tive frame, the drawing will be slightly different to indicate
motion taking place. It takes twenty-four frames to equal one
minute of animation. After the cels are finished and colored in,
they are filmed with a movie camera. Each cel is filmed as one frame of film. When all

A pen plotter is a
sort of printer with a pen
attached to a mechanical arm.
The arm moves according to
the coordinates programmed
into the computer.

the frames are projected onto a screen one after another, the characters in the cel drawings appear to move.

The first attempts at computer animation took place at research institutes in the early 1960s. The most important breakthroughs were produced at Boeing and at the Mathematical Applications Group (MAGI). Researchers there created these early animations on expensive mainframe computers. Mainframes were huge—they sometimes took up a whole room—and were very slow compared to today's personal computers. Users worked at terminals: monitors that were connected to the mainframe computer.

Two engineers, William Fetter and Walter Bernhart, created several short animations at Boeing. One showed the steps in the landing of an aircraft carrier. It was created by printing a series of three-dimensional drawings by hand, then filming these drawings one at a time.

MAGI was the first commercial company to create computer animations with fully rendered polygonal objects. This

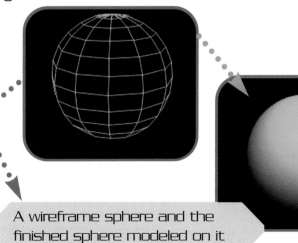

A wireframe sphere and the finished sphere modeled on it

was done by coloring 3-D objects, which were created using many three-sided planes. Up until this point, all computer animation looked like pencil drawings.

Significant advances in three-dimensional computer animations came about in the 1970s. During this decade, a number of basic rendering (creating) techniques were created that are still used today. These included techniques for image- and bump-texture mapping: the process of placing a two-dimensional image, such as a photograph, onto a three-dimensional object, like a cube. Facial animations—the process of making the character talk—were also invented around this time. David Evans of the University of Utah led these advances.

Another major influence in computer animation technology was Ohio State University's Computer Graphics Research Group. This group was directed by Charles Csuri. Ohio State University developed several real-time and non-real-time systems. Real-time systems can change the image on the screen at the same time that you move the mouse. A non-real-time system cannot. It takes a few seconds, minutes, or hours for the updated image to appear on the screen.

William Fetter coined the term "computer graphics" in the 1960s.

In the 1980s, computer animation moved out of the research institutes and into the real world. The computer industry began to take off, and affordable computer workstations, minicomputers, and personal computers made it possible for commercial animation houses to become successful. These companies included Robert Abel Associates, Digital Effects, Cranston-Csuri, and Pacific Data Images (PDI).

During the 1980s, people at Ohio State continued to perform research and development in computer graphics. Along with researchers at Cornell University, they refined and expanded on techniques in the areas of hierarchical character animation (how the models that make up a human figure are grouped together so that when animated, the body moves correctly); inverse kinematics (the process by which an object is animated by positioning its lowest level (for example, move the hand and the whole arm follows); and motion dynamics (commands that simulate such things as gravity, wind, and collision).

CREATIVE MILESTONES ▶▶▶▶▶

When you watch science fiction and action adventure movies from the '80s and '90s you can see the growth of computer animation and special effects. The *Alien* movies are a good example. *Alien* was released in 1979, and the

The most recent *Star Wars* film used computer animation almost exclusively.

most recent, *Alien: Resurrection,* was released in 1997. If you watch the two movies in the order they were released, you can see how much more sophisticated the technology has become and how much better the effects are now blending with the live action.

Another example is the *Star Wars* saga. The original trilogy incorporated computer special effects, stop motion animation (filming the motion frame-by-frame while changing the position of the object slightly), and animatronics (life-size remote-controlled puppets) along with traditional special effects. Those three movies were very advanced for their time. But the most recent film, *Star Wars: The Phantom Menace,* used computer animations and computerized special effects almost exclusively.

Although these later installments look slicker than their earlier counterparts, the first films introduced groundbreaking techniques. There was nothing quite like them at the time, which is one reason that the films were so popular.

The 1970s ▶▶▶▶▶▶▶▶

As mentioned earlier, people first created computer-aided animations as early as the 1960s. These early efforts were created by scientists and engineers who had little or no artistic background. They were more interested in the scientific process of computer animation—how to make the computer do what was necessary to create animations—than the creative process.

Advances in computer technology in the 1970s brought advances in computer animation and special effects. Most of the notable works during this decade were commercials created for advertising agencies. But in 1975, George Lucas founded his visual effects company, Industrial

George Lucas is the founder of the visual effects company Industrial Light and Magic.

Light and Magic (ILM), which cre-
ated the special effects for *Star
Wars, Raiders of the Lost Ark,
Jurassic Park,* and most recently,
*Star Wars: The Phantom
Menace* and *The Mummy.*

ILM is one of the most
creative and influential
visual effects companies
ever, and it domi-
nates the industry.
Other important

Disney's *TRON* was a milestone in the
use of computer animation in film.

companies include Pixar, PDI, Rhythm and Hues, Digital
Domain, and Blue Sky/ViFX.

The 1980s ▶▶▶▶▶▶▶▶▶

It was the 1980s that truly saw the rise of animation pro-
jects. In 1982, Disney's *TRON* was the first movie to
include more than twenty minutes of computer animation,
some of which was composited (mixed in) with live action
footage. *The Last Starfighter* by Digital Productions was the
first feature film to include computer animation segments
featuring highly realistic and detailed models.

Pixar, founded by Apple Computer's Steve Jobs,
created some inspirational and amusing character animation

shorts in the late 1980s. With an animation team led by John Lasseter, Pixar produced animations *Luxo, Jr* (1985); *Red's Dream* (1987); *Tin Toy* (1988); which won an Academy Award for Best Animated Short Film; and *Knickknack* (1989). You may never have heard of any of these movies, but they were important because of their technical quality and because they proved that traditional animation principles could be applied to computer-generated animation.

In 1989 the feature film *The Abyss* seamlessly combined three-dimensional computer animation with live action using computer systems and programs that could be bought in any computer store.

The 1990s ▶▶▶▶▶▶▶▶▶

Computer animation and special effects have become increasingly sophisticated in the 1990s, beginning with the 1991 film *Terminator II,* with effects by ILM. This was the first film to use

Jurassic Park is a standout among recent computer-animated films.

computer graphics to simulate natural human motion. Some of the other standout movies of the 1990s included *Jurassic Park, Titanic,* and *Babe.*

Recent television commercials have contained excellent three-dimensional computer animation as well. These include Coca-Cola's polar bears, among many others.

However, the greatest feat of the decade was the Walt Disney film *Toy Story,* with effects by Pixar. This was the first three-dimensional full-length feature ani-

Toy Story was computer animation's greatest achievement in the 1990s.

mation created entirely on computers, without any conventional animation.

With each new year and new project, computer animation firms take the technology further and further. Do you want to be one of the people who decides what computer animations of the future will look like? If you have an interest in art, a talent for drawing and storytelling, and some computer skills, the exciting world of computer animation might be just right for you.

chapter two

THE USES OF COMPUTER ANIMATION

Computer animations incorporate everything from flying logos to digital stuntpeople. Special effects range from photorealism, in which animations look like real objects and characters (*Titanic* is one example of this) to fantasy (such as *A Bug's Life*).

The use of computer animation in the media (means of communication) includes broadcast animation, television animation, feature film animation, and visual effects for movies and television.

BROADCAST ANIMATION ▶▶▶

Broadcast (or on-air computer graphics) is the oldest medium for computer animation and has expanded with the growth of cable and satellite television.

With an emphasis on design, this medium uses the computer to create animation and special effects for news-related shows and documentaries. It even includes on-air promotions (advertising and publicity) for TV networks.

The Discovery Channel, a cable TV network, produces many shows that utilize computer animations to re-create events for which no live film or video footage is available. For example, their series on dinosaurs incorporates many computer animations to demonstrate how dinosaurs looked, moved, and hunted.

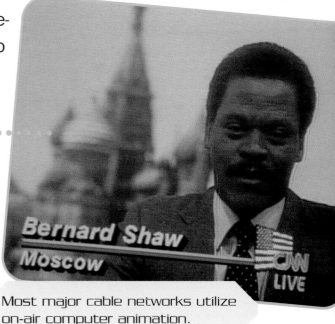

Most major cable networks utilize on-air computer animation.

Television producers may also use broadcast animation to show the details of how an airplane crashed, how a ship sank, or how germs multiply—as just a few examples—for a news segment or special. Since these types of things are hard to re-create or demonstrate any other way, computer animation is a perfect medium with which to show them.

TELEVISION ANIMATION ▶▶▶▶

Computer-generated animation for television combines the techniques of traditional animation with computer technology. Some obvious examples of TV animation include Comedy Central's *South Park* and the cartoons that air on Saturday mornings.

Traditional animation techniques are extremely time-consuming.

The computer helps maintain the quality and look of traditional anima- tion. But creat- ing traditional animation can be a slow process, and television programs usually have to be produced in a short time. Computer animations can be created much more quickly, so they are ideal for television productions. To be in this field, you must be able to work at a very fast pace but with great care and atten- tion to detail. The animations must be done just right to fit the look of the program or series.

Computers are used for both two- and three-dimensional

animation. In two-dimensional animations, the frames are drawn onto cels. These cels are then scanned into the computer. There an artist colors them and uses the computer to transfer the cels to videotape. There are also a growing number of shows, such as *The Adventures of Johnny Quest,* that combine two- and three-dimensional animation, and others that are entirely three-dimensional, such as *Reboot.* With the advances in computer hardware and software and the popularity of prime-time animated shows, many more are bound to come.

FEATURE FILM ANIMATION ▶▶▶▶

Snow White and the Seven Dwarfs, Cinderella, and *Bambi*—most of us grew up with these classic animated Disney films. When these movies were created, all the animations were drawn and inked by hand. Today with the advent of computers, computer animations can be used in a single scene or throughout an entire film.

The computer has helped animators by taking over some of the complex tasks and details that would be next to impossible to do by hand. For the past several years, Disney has turned to computers to create some of its most difficult scenes. The fight scene in *Hercules* between Hercules and the dragon is one example. Each time Hercules beheads the dragon, it grows two new heads, and this goes on until it has grown at least thirty. This character would have been very difficult and time con-suming for a tradi-tional animator to tackle by hand. So the dragon was modeled and ani-mated on the computer and then inte-grated with

Contemporary films are heavily reliant upon computer animation.

the rest of the elements in the scene. Other examples of this process include the flying carpet in *Aladdin,* the wilde-beest stampede in *The Lion King,* and the crowd scenes in *The Hunchback of Notre Dame.*

In 1995 feature film animations became fully computerized—and revolutionized. Disney and Pixar's *Toy Story* was the first full-length, entirely three-dimensional computer feature film animation. Directed by John Lasseter, *Toy Story* took five years to complete and received an Academy Award nomination for Best Picture.

This was followed by two more three-dimensional feature film animations, *Antz* (produced by Dreamworks Pictures, with animation by PDI) and Walt Disney and Pixar's *A Bug's Life*. Both were released in 1998. We can be sure that the success of these films will lead to many more in the same style, including the sequel to *Toy Story*.

VISUAL EFFECTS ▶▶▶▶

When you think of visual effects, you may immediately think of *Star Wars,* with its dazzling fantasy worlds and alien creatures, or perhaps *Twister*, with exploding buildings and flying cars and livestock. But visual effects include much more than these obvious examples.

This area of computer animation includes visual effects not only for feature films but also for TV commercials, motion-based rides, video games, and even music videos.

It's true that the most recognizable form of visual effects is in films such as *Star Wars,* where entire worlds are created inside the computer and later meshed with live-action footage, movies such as *Men in Black,* in which real humans interact with computer-created creatures, or films such as *Titanic,* in which the effects are created to blend with the live action so that you can't tell one from the other.

Filmmakers rely on computers for these types of visual effects because it would be difficult (or even impossible) and costly to create them in the real world.

Computers can also create digital stuntmen:

Motion-based rides often feature computer-animated special effects.

animations of human characters that perform stunts too dangerous for a human to do. One of the first films to use digital stuntpeople was *Batman.* Visual effects are used to create talking animals as well.

Television commercials also rely on visual effects. Advertisers use visual effects to sell everything from automobiles to telephone companies, from cereal to fast food.

Many different areas of film and television use computer animation in one form or another. The more sophisticated the available computer hardware and software become, the more uses for computer animation there will be.

chapter three

WHAT COMPUTER ANIMATORS DO

Every computer animation project goes through three phases: preproduction, production, and post-production. Each of these phases requires different skills. Every animation firm has its own definition of what has to be done at each stage. In large companies, employees may work on only one or two stages, whereas in small companies, each employee is likely to be involved at each stage.

PREPRODUCTION ▶▶▶▶▶▶▶▶▶▶

This phase of the animation process usually revolves around the idea behind the project. During this stage, writers create the script, including the dialogue that the characters and the narrator will speak. Actors are hired to provide the characters' and narrator's voices, which may be recorded during this stage. Artists create storyboards and design layouts.

Storyboard Artist ▶▶▶▶▶▶▶▶▶▶

A storyboard artist translates the written script into two-dimensional images. Working closely with the director, writer, and production staff, the storyboard artist then revises these drawings during story sessions until everyone is happy with the final product. Storyboard artists have training and skills in illustration or fine art. It is important for these artists to show a flair for action and expression and to have the skill to exaggerate a pose or perspective.

A storyboard shows the key actions for each scene. Artists usually draw storyboards in two dimensions.

Story Concept and Design ▶▶▶▶▶▶▶▶▶

The person who holds this position, also known as the art director, designs the overall look and tone of the animation. What type of visual style will the animations have? Will they be highly realistic like *Tarzan,* or will they take on a stylized cartoon look such as *The Simpsons?* The art director determines the look of the background setting—

Panel 1 Panel 2 Panel 3 Panel 4 Panel 5 Panel 6 Panel 7 Panel 8 Panel 9

Animation begins with the ideas of the storyboard artist.

the locations and time period. These people create everything you will eventually see on the screen. Like storyboard artists, people in these positions are usually illustrators or fine artists.

People who work in concept and design must have not only artistic skill but also the ability to research using reference material. For example, Disney sent its staff on a safari before they worked on *The Lion King.* This opportunity to observe animals in the wild and look at a real jungle environment helped them make the animals in the film more realistic.

Also during the concept and design stage, characters are physically created by turning detailed drawings into three-dimensional models sculpted out of clay. These models are then scanned into computers to create 3-D computer digital models. Sculptors are hired to create these models.

Layout Artist ▶▶▶▶▶▶▶▶▶

The layout artist translates each storyboard frame into one or more composed shots. He or she composes the scene by putting each element in its place. The frames are then filmed to create an animatic. The layout artist also positions cameras, characters, sets, and lights.

An animatic is a film of the storyboard images. Each panel is held for the length of time that the scene will take onscreen.

Layout artists generally need to have training or experience in both fine arts and computer graphics. Most layout artists work at large firms. The position doesn't exist at most smaller companies.

PRODUCTION ▶▶▶▶▶▶▶▶

During the production process, various people do the actual work of producing the animation. Characters are modeled and brought to life.

Technical Director ▶▶▶▶▶▶▶▶▶

Technical directors (TDs) build the characters and sets that will be used in the animation. They model everything, from the hair on the character's head to the shoes on its feet to the house that the character lives in to the street that the house is on.

To model the character properly, the TD has to have an idea of what the character will be expected to do over the course of the animation. For example, if the character is a tin soldier, it will not need as much movement in its legs and arms as a dancer would. Those two models would be created differently from each other. Other things to consider include the distance from the camera (which will help determine the complexity of the model), the style of animation (cartoony or photorealistic), and the type of character (hero or villain, old or young, etc.).

At smaller companies, a TD may also create tex- tures; position lights; do character setup, which involves creating the bone structure used to ani- mate the model;

TDs create models for everything to be used in the animation.

and even develop software to use in the production of the animation.This position requires lots of computer experience as well as a fine-arts background. A background in computer programming or architecture is also helpful.

Observing real life will make your animation look more convincing.

Animator ▶▶▶▶

The animator is the heart and soul of any animation project. The animator's job is to bring the illusion of life to all inanimate (nonmoving) objects. This includes anything from making the lead character walk across the room to making it lip-sync to the actor's voice, from animating a barking dog to making a door swing open—and having it all look convincing.

Important aspects of animation include the timing of an action, the weight of an object, and techniques such as squash and stretch—exaggerated motion used to demonstrate the force of motion—which are carried over from 2-D animation. These aspects are important because our brains can detect when an object doesn't appear to be moving correctly.

The position of animator demands attention to detail, a strong sense of how creatures move, and artistic skill. A background in fine arts and computer graphics is also needed.

Special-Effects Animator ▶▶▶▶▶▶▶▶▶▶

This type of animator creates natural and fantasy effects, such as those involving water, fire, tornadoes, sand, smoke, or fireworks. A special-effects animator created the sandstorm in *The Mummy,* the tornadoes in *Twister,* and the lava in *Volcano.* A background in graphic design is needed for this position, and an interest in physics and natural science is very helpful.

Texture Mapping ▶▶▶▶▶▶▶▶▶

Texture mapping includes creating anything from the color of a shirt to the bark of a tree. It is somewhat like hanging wallpaper or wrapping a present. The texture mapper creates a 2-D drawing of the texture and wraps it onto a three-dimensional model.

Special effects animators need to have training in graphic design.

For this position, a fine-art background is extremely helpful. So is experience with computer imaging and drawing programs such as Photoshop and Illustrator.

Lighting ▶▶▶▶▶▶▶▶▶▶

Lighting creates the mood of the scenes and can help tell the story. Lighting design is generally done after the models have been designed, the animation completed, and texture maps and cameras placed. The way a character is lit can tell the viewer something about that character. A character shown almost all in shadow, for example, can suggest that the character has a secret or that there is something sinister about him or her. It can give the viewer information about the time of day or show the passage of time. A background in photography and film is very useful for this position, in addition to experience with and knowledge of computers.

Programming ▶▶▶▶▶▶▶▶▶▶

In an animation studio, computer programmers create new software tools or modify existing ones. For example, if the special-effects animator wants a character to perform a certain yoga move, but the computer software doesn't allow the character's joint to bend in that particular way, a programmer will write or rewrite a program that will allow the animator to make the character move that way. Programmers may do their job at different times during the production process. This position requires a strong background in computer programming, usually including a college degree in computer science and previous programming experience.

Programming requires a strong background in computer science.

POSTPRODUCTION ▶▶▶▶▶▶▶▶▶

When all the animation is completed and artists have rendered final versions of all the scenes, postproduction begins. Postproduction includes compositing (blending or combining) the elements of a single frame together and editing the scenes to create a complete project.

Compositing ▶▶▶▶▶▶▶▶▶

A compositing technician combines all the pieces that make up a single frame. For example, the technician might create a mask to delete the blue screen that was used as a background during filming. A mask is an image, like a stencil that protects the part of the picture that is to remain unchanged with a transparent color, usually red. It is created by selecting or painting over the unwanted areas or the frame. This area is replaced with the images created in the computer. Then the compositing technician might take the image and add an explosion. This process would be repeated for every frame in the scene. This position requires a background in and experience with computer technology, especially the software that is used in compositing.

Digital Editing ▶▶▶▶

Scenes are not always filmed in the same order in which they will appear in the final version of the animation, so they need to be arranged correctly when they

Digital editors put all of a film's scenes together seamlessly.

are all completed. An editor puts all the scenes together in order and creates the transitions from one scene to the next. You've probably noticed that in films, TV programs, and even video games, scenes change in different ways. Some scenes end with a fade to black, in which the image disappears completely before the next scene appears. Another common transition is a dissolve, in which one scene gradually blends into the next.

This position requires training in and experience with film or video editing, using either traditional editing equipment or computer-editing software.

chapter four

GET THE
KNOW-HOW

It takes more than just the desire to be an animator to get a job in this field. You need to have artistic talent, computer ability, and the willingness to continually improve your skills and learn new ones.

To obtain a job at any animation company, you'll need a college degree in art, preferably with a concentration in one or more of the following subjects: illustration, sculpture, traditional animation, computer animation and graphics, or programming. Although computer skills and programming ability are helpful, they are not essential. Many animation firms hire extremely talented artists, illustrators, and sculptors and train them to use the necessary computer software and hardware. Computer programs can be learned, but it's more important to have some basic art skills such as life drawing and

Basic Drawing Skills

These are some of the basic items that you should practice drawing to develop your drawing skills.

- life drawing
- figures and animals in motion
- fantasy design
- architecture
- landscapes and environments
- perspective
- facial expressions

photography. When you're job-hunting, you will highlight your artistic skills in a portfolio and on a demo reel (a sample film or videotape), which will be reviewed by the firms that are hiring.

WHAT YOU CAN DO NOW ▶▶▶▶▶

If you're interested in animation but think that college seems a long way off, fear not. There are many things you can do in the meantime to prepare for a career in computer animation.

Basic Drawing Skills ▶▶▶▶▶▶▶▶▶▶

If you can draw, even just a little, it is important to perfect some basic drawing skills like anatomy, perspective, and landscapes.

You can do this by participating in your school's art classes or art club. There you will be able to practice, learn how to use various tools (for example, paint, watercolor, and colored pencils), and get some helpful feedback from your instructors.

Art classes are excellent preparation for a career in animation.

It is also a good idea to study master painters such as van Gogh, da Vinci, and Picasso. Good sources for this are local museums and books from your school or local library.

Composition and Storytelling Skills

All good animators need to be good storytellers. They need to know how to develop a story, how to keep it moving along in an interesting way, and how to make it visually appealing and exciting to the audience.

A great way to study this is to watch animations, including cartoons and films. Any type of film is helpful, but some of the best filmmakers include Alfred Hitchcock,

Steven Spielberg, and Orson Welles. Welles's *Citizen Kane* is generally thought to be one of the finest examples of film. It encompasses some excellent examples of composition, lighting, and storytelling. In addition, Walt Disney animations, Betty Boop cartoons, Warner Brothers (especially those by Chuck Jones) cartoons, and Japanese animations are good sources for understanding the basics of traditional animation. Key concepts in computer animation, such as squash and stretch, exaggerated action, anticipation (a short movement leading up to a major action—for example, a character hanging in midair before falling), and ease in and ease out (in which a character's actions begin slowly, get up to full speed, and then slowly end), all have their roots in traditional animation.

Comic books such as *Batman, Superman,* and *Spiderman,* are also great study guides for how to compose a scene and how to tell a story visually. The basics of a good storyboard can be learned from

Comic books are great study guides for scene composition and storytelling.

comic books. In addition, you can get ideas about interesting camera framing and angles and apply them to animation.

People-Watching ▶▶▶▶▶▶▶▶▶▶

Observing is another good way to prepare for learning computer animation. You can watch not just people but anything that moves. Watch how different people walk. Everyone walks differently, from the toddler just learning to walk to the elderly man who uses a cane to assist him. Watch people's facial expressions. How do their faces look when they smile or frown? Notice the slight details in muscle movement when someone smiles—how the ends of the mouth curl, the cheeks bulge slightly, and the eyebrows raise. Subtle details like these make all the difference in bringing a character to life. Also, the weight of an object is important. A rubber ball, for example, bounces differently from a bowling ball or a beach ball.

Studying everything around you and paying attention to the little details—from insects to animals, from cars to falling leaves—can help you become a great animator.

Attending Conferences ▶▶▶▶▶▶▶▶

Special Interest Group on Computer Graphics (SIGGRAPH) is an organization of the Association for Computing Machinery (ACM). ACM is the oldest educational and scientific computing society in the world. SIGGRAPH was founded in 1967. It began with a small group of computer graphic enthusiasts and has now expanded its membership to include artists, engineers, animators, filmmakers, software and hardware developers, scientists, mathematicians, and other professionals in the field of computer graphics.

Each year SIGGRAPH hosts the biggest conference on computer animation in the country. There computer animation professionals gather to share information and techniques and to showcase their latest pieces. The conference includes an event geared toward education professionals and students of all levels. The SIGGRAPH conference in 1998 featured an event called sigKIDS, which showcased animations and interactive multimedia pieces created by kids in grades three through twelve.

The most exciting event by far is the Computer Animation Festival Electronic Theater. Here SIGGRAPH

The SIGGRAPH conference is an excellent place to see what's happening in the field.

screens the year's finest, most innovative, and most techni-
cally challenging animations, motion picture effects, and scientific breakthroughs. Attending the conference is a great
way to meet and talk with professionals in the field and get
a feel for what the industry is all about.

In addition to the annual conference, SIGGRAPH has a
network of professional chapters in various cities around the
world, including two for students: one college and one high
school chapter. For more information, check out its Web site
at *http://www.siggraph.org*.

chapter five

BEYOND Y2K

As mentioned in the first chapter, most early computer animation was performed by scientists and engineers who had little or no artistic background. Today this is not the case. Yes, there are still a lot of scientists and engineers in the field, but they work in the research and development areas of the industry. Computer animators have some kind of an artistic background, whether in computer art or traditional fine art.

The computer animation industry is becoming very specialized. This means that most large animation houses hire employees to do one specific step or task in the animation process. An artist hired as a lighting technician would not perform any character animation, and a character animator would not set up lighting for a scene.

In addition, many companies in the industry hire a large number of freelancers: people who work on a project-by-project basis. These employees work only until they have completed the project and then move on to other companies or assignments.

Another change in the industry, one that is expected to become more common in the future, is large companies hiring smaller companies to take on part or all of a job. This is called "sourcing out" or "farming out" work. The film *Titanic,* for example, had too many elaborate special effects for one company to complete by the deadline. Although one company, Digital Domain, created the bulk of the effects, four separate companies shared information back and forth, each working on a different part of the project, to create the

Titanic used several different computer animating companies for its special effects.

effects for this film. As the demand for computer animation grows, more companies will farm out some of their work.

With the success and popularity of films such as *Toy*

Story, Antz, and *A Bug's Life,* feature films will incorporate more and more three-dimensional animation. Skills and experience with this type of animation will become increasingly

The popularity of films such as *Antz* shows no signs of slowing down.

important. Maybe you'll become an expert in three-dimensional animation and create effects that will amaze the world.

WORDS.COM: GLOSSARY

animatic   A preliminary version of the animation by filming each panel of the storyboard for the length of time that that scene will appear on screen.

animation   The art of movement, which gives life to inanimate objects.

animatronics   Realistic life-size, remote-controlled puppets.

cel   A piece of clear plastic material on which an animator draws a single frame of an animation.

compositing   Combining two or more images to create a single image.

computer graphics   Any graphic image created with the aid of a computer.

frame   A single still image in an animation. Twenty-four frames create one second of animation.

lip-synch   Moving a character's lips in time with the soundtrack of an animation.

live action   Footage shot in the real world using real characters and sets.

mask   A piece of film or other overlay that covers the desired area of an image. Masks are translucent and are usually red.

polygon   A surface, for example a sphere, defined by three or more edges and three or more points. The simplest polygon is a triangle.

render   The process in which the computer creates a final two-dimensional image from the three-dimensional data, such as lighting and shading.

stop motion animation   Animation created by recording one frame of film, stopping the camera, making changes to the scene, and shooting another frame of film.

storyboard   A series of drawings that illustrate the key actions, ideas, and arrangements of each scene in an animation.

traditional animation   Animation created by drawing each frame by hand on a cel.

turnkey system   A commercially available software product that is created, distributed, and maintained by a vendor and can be used on compatible computer platforms.

RESOURCES.COM: WEB SITES

Computer Graphics
http://mambo.ucsc.edu/psl/cg.mpg

Computer Graphics and Animation
http://www.bergen.org/AAST/ComputerAnimation

The East Coast Digital Consortium
http://www.ecdc.com

SIGGRAPH
http://www.siggraph.org

3-D Site
http://www.3dsite.com

Women in Animation
http://women.in.animation.org

World Internet Animation
http://www.animation.org

BOOKS.COM:
FOR FURTHER READING

Baker, Christopher W. *Let There Be Life! Animating with the Computer.* New York: Walker Publishing Co., 1997.

Blair, Preston. *How to Animate Film Cartoons.* Laguna Hills, CA: Walter Foster Publishing, 1989.

Kerlow, Isaac V. *The Art of 3-D Computer Animation and Imaging.* New York: John Wiley & Sons, 1996.

Kettlekamp, Larry. *Computer Graphics: How It Works, What It Does.* New York: William Morrow & Co., Inc., 1989.

Lewinter, Renee. *Web Animation for Dummies.* Indianapolis, IN: IDG Books Worldwide, 1997.

Locke, Lafe. *Making "Movies" Without a Camera.* Cincinnati: F & W Publications, 1992.

Maestri, George. *Digital Character Animation.* Indianapolis, IN: New Riders Publishing, 1996.

Muybridge, Eadweard. *The Human Figure in Motion.* Mineola, New York: Dover Publications, 1955.

Street, Rita. *Computer Animation: A Whole New World.* Gloucester, MA: Rockport Publishers, 1998.

INDEX

CREDITS

ABOUT THE AUTHOR

Annie O'Donnell holds a master's degree in computer graphics and interactive multimedia from Pratt Institute in Brooklyn, New York. Her thesis included a two-minute 3-D computer animation. She lives and works in New York City.

PHOTO CREDITS

LAYOUT AND DESIGN
Annie O'Donnell

Consulting Editor
Amy Haugesag